Benito MUSSOLINI

DAVID DOWNING

Heinemann
LIBRARY

www.heinemann.co.uk/library

Visit our website to find out more information about Heinemann Library books.

To order:
 Phone 44 (0) 1865 888066
Send a fax to 44 (0) 1865 314091
Visit the Heinemann Bookshop at www.heinemann.co.uk/library to browse our catalogue and order online.

First published in Great Britain by Heinemann Library,
Halley Court, Jordan Hill, Oxford OX2 8EJ,
a division of Reed Educational and Professional Publishing Ltd.
Heinemann is a registered trademark of Reed Educational and Professional Publishing Ltd.

OXFORD MELBOURNE AUCKLAND
JOHANNESBURG BLANTYRE GABORONE
IBADAN PORTSMOUTH (NH) USA CHICAGO

Designed by AMR
Illustrated by Art Construction
Originated by Dot Gradations
Printed in China

ISBN 0 431 13850 8
05 04 03 02 01
10 9 8 7 6 5 4 3 2 1

British Library Cataloguing in Publication Data
Downing, David
 Benito Mussolini. – (Leading lives)
 1.Mussolini, Benito – Juvenile literature 2.Heads of state
 – Italy – Biography – Juvenile literature 3.Dictators –
 Italy – Biography – Juvenile literature 4.World War,
 1939–1945 – Germany – Juvenile literature 5.Fascists –
 Italy – Juvenile literature 6.Italy – Politics and
 govenment – 1933–1945 – Juvenile literature
 I.Title
 945'.091'092

Acknowledgements
The publishers would like to thank the following for permission to reproduce photographs:
AKG: pp.24, 26, 27, 30, 45; Hulton Getty: pp. 4, 6, 8, 9, 13, 16, 18, 29, 31, 33, 39, 40, 43, 47, 48, 51, 52;
Imperial War Museum: p. 7; Mary Evans: pp. 23, 54; PA Photos: p. 19; Popperfoto: pp.17, 44, 53; University of Wisconsin: p. 35.

Cover photograph reproduced with permission of Hulton Getty.

Our thanks to Christopher Gibb for his comments in the preparation for this book.

Every effort has been made to contact copyright holders of any material reproduced in this book. Any omissions will be rectified in subsequent printings if notice is given to the publishers.

Any words appearing in the text in bold, **like this**, are explained in the Glossary.

Contents

'Duce!'

The year is 1936. It is just before 10.30 on a warm spring evening in Rome, the capital of Italy. A bright moon shines down on the huge restless crowd of almost 400,000 people, which fills the square and overflows down the nearby streets. There are shouts of excitement.

▲ Benito Mussolini, il Duce, *acknowledging the cheers of a large crowd from the Palazzo Venezia in Rome.*

The doors to the balcony on the first floor of the palace are opening – a man is stepping out. The roar of the crowd fills the air. The man looks down at the adoring faces. He is wearing a black shirt, a grey uniform, a black cap – the Fascist uniform. He has his hands on his hips, his chin thrust forward, his legs planted like trees trunks. It is the way he always stands.

He lifts a hand and the roar of the crowd dies away almost instantly. All over Italy other crowds are gathered in town and village squares, their eyes on the loudspeakers which will broadcast his every word. He tells them, in that deep voice they love so much, that the Italian army has won its war in Abyssinia. 'Every knot has been cut by our shining sword,' he says. 'Italy has her Empire.' There is wild cheering from the crowd, cheering that goes on and on as he stares down at the sea of faces, no expression on his face.

This is *il Duce*, the leader. His name is Benito Mussolini, and he is now 52 years old. It has been sixteen years since he introduced his new doctrine of Fascism to Italy and the world; thirteen years since he took power in Rome, turning Italy into a **dictatorship**. For many he can do no wrong. He is described by some as the 'rightful heir of Caesar' and 'the man of the century'. He is said to be greater than Washington, Lincoln or Napoleon. Some even say that he has halted the flow of lava from a volcano by sheer force of will, and so saved a village. He seems more like a god than a man.

'*Duce! Duce! Duce!* [Leader! Leader! Leader!]' the crowd chants, filling the sky above Rome with their love and adoration.

Where has this man come from? What has he done in those thirteen years of power to make himself so popular? And why, nine years from now, will his own people shoot him, and jeer at his body as it hangs by the heels in a square just like this one?

Childhood and youth

To locate the places mentioned, see the map of Italy on page 10.

▲ *The building in Dovia where Benito Mussolini was born. His family lived on the second floor.*

Benito Mussolini was born in the tiny village of Dovia, in the Romagna region of northern Italy, on 29 July 1883. He was the first of three children born to Allesandro and Rosa Mussolini. Two years later they had another son, Arnaldo, and four years after that a daughter, Edvige. Like most Italians the Mussolinis were Catholics, although Rosa was much more religious than Allesandro.

Allesandro was a **blacksmith**, but he spent more time drinking and arguing about politics than working. Rosa was the village schoolteacher, and the family lived in two rooms on the second floor of the school house. They were not rich, but they were better off than most in this poor area of the country. Food was simple but plentiful, and there were many books for the young Benito to read.

He was often disobedient, and quick to lose his temper. He frequently got into fights with other children. His father, who regularly beat Benito's mother, often used a thick leather strap on the young boy, but these punishments only seemed to make him more rebellious.

School days

At the age of 9 Benito was sent away to a Catholic boarding school, where it was hoped he would learn to behave better. He hated the strict discipline and the rich boys who sat at a different table and were given better food. He refused to do his school work and he bullied the other boys. In one fight he stabbed his opponent with his penknife.

His parents sent him to a different school, where he stabbed another boy. The headmaster's first instinct was to expel Benito, but he had noticed the intelligence beneath the boy's anger, and decided to let him stay on. Benito learned to control himself a little better, and as the years went by he discovered a hunger for knowledge and a love of speaking out loud. He used to stand on the hills above his village and recite poems in his powerful voice. He was already interested in politics, and drawn to **Socialist** ideas, influenced both by his father and his own anger at injustice.

Leaving home

'On the day before we started I had quarrelled with a companion and had tried to hit him but missed and my fist went smash against a wall and I hurt my knuckles so badly that I had to leave with my hand bandaged up. At the moment of parting I cried.'

(Mussolini, writing about the day he first left home for school)

◀ Benito's parents. Allesandro was a blacksmith, Rosa was the village schoolteacher.

At the age of 18 Mussolini passed his final exams and gained a teaching diploma, much to the delight of his mother. But his first job as a teacher only lasted four months. The local council had hired him because they agreed with his politics, but the children's parents disliked his drinking, his card-playing and his love affair with a woman whose soldier husband was away on duty.

The wide world
When the job ended he travelled north to Switzerland. He wanted to avoid **military service**, which he did not agree with, and also wanted to see more of the world. The first few months were hard. He slept in the open and often had to beg for food. When he got work the pay was often very low. But he was better educated than most of his fellow-workers and he soon found better jobs, writing for a Socialist newspaper and organizing **propaganda** for a **trade union**.

He read and wrote a great deal, and spent a lot of time in passionate arguments. He called himself an '**authoritarian Communist**', and looked forward to a violent revolution in which parliament and private property would both be abolished. These views did not make him very popular with the authorities in Switzerland and he was eventually ordered to leave the country.

3 The Socialist

Mussolini spent most of the next year wandering around the countries near Italy, doing odd jobs, learning other languages, reading lots of books, writing poetry and political articles. In 1904 the Italian government offered to pardon those who had evaded **military service** if they agreed to join up now, and Mussolini, who was perhaps a little homesick, decided to take advantage of the offer.

A cry from the heart

'Look! People eating, drinking and enjoying themselves. And I will travel third class, eat miserable cheap food... . How I hate the rich! Why must I suffer this injustice? How long must we wait?'

(Mussolini in Switzerland, 1904)

▶ Benito Mussolini, in a pose taken around 1904.

Teacher

Mussolini helped his mother with her teaching for a few months and then joined his army unit. A year later his mother died and he seemed overcome with grief, although he had never been very kind to her when she was alive. When he was released from the army in September 1906 he took another teaching job in the far north of Italy, close to the border with the **Austro-Hungarian Empire**. He seems to have lost his interest in politics for a while, but his behaviour was as bad as ever. His pupils thought he was mad and their parents objected to his drinking and affairs with women. He was not asked to stay when the school year ended.

Back home in the Romagna, he passed an exam which allowed him to teach French in secondary school. It looked for a while as if he was going to leave his angry politics behind, but during his next teaching job he was offered the position of **editor** for a local **Socialist** magazine, and his political passions were re-awakened.

◀ Italy c. 1910.

When he returned home in the following summer he became involved in a bitter dispute between landowners and part-time farm workers, and ended up serving a short prison sentence.

Journalist

His next job was editing a Socialist newspaper in the Trentino, a north Italian region that was still part of the Austro-Hungarian Empire. Mussolini learned a lot about running a newspaper, but his violent writing and behaviour soon got him into trouble with the authorities. He was sent to prison more than once and his paper was confiscated several times. After seven months he was sent back to Italy.

Before leaving for the Trentino Mussolini had become engaged to Rachele Guidi, one of the daughters of his father's new companion, Anna. He had not sent Rachele a single postcard during his time away, but when he returned to the Romagna he asked permission to live with her. When the couple's parents refused he threatened to shoot himself, and got his way. He and Rachele eventually married, and had five children.

Mussolini supported his growing family with a new job in nearby Forli, editing another Socialist magazine. His views were still **anti-establishment**, **anti-clerical** and **anti-militaristic**, and much too extreme for most people. Then the Italian government decided to conquer Libya in North Africa, a policy that Mussolini violently opposed. His organization of factory closures and railway **sabotage** in Forli made him a national celebrity. After serving several months in prison he was invited to Milan to edit *Avanti!* (*Forward!*), the most important Socialist newspaper in Italy.

Mussolini and his growing family moved to Milan. He was a success as the **editor** of *Avanti!*, more than doubling its readership in his two years at the newspaper. He wrote many of the articles himself and his bold attacks on government and **business leaders** were very popular. In private he was less of a revolutionary. One of his girlfriends noticed that he did his best to look poor and dirty when speaking to an audience, but changed back into smart clothes after the meeting. She also noticed that he often changed his mind during a conversation to agree with what the last person had said.

His most famous change of mind came in 1914. When World War I started in August, Italy stayed **neutral**, and most Italian **Socialists**, including Mussolini, thought it should remain so. But as the weeks went by his own love of drama and action pushed him in the opposite direction. By November he was arguing that Italy could not afford to be left out of such an important conflict. He resigned from *Avanti!* and set up another newspaper, *Il Popolo d'Italia* (*The Italian People*), which he said was both pro-Socialist and pro-war.

▼ *Mussolini being arrested during a pro-war demonstration.*

Soldier

When Italy entered the war in 1915 Mussolini did not immediately volunteer to fight. He was eventually called up in September, and spent over a year on Italy's frontier with Austria–Hungary. Life in the **trenches** was mostly either miserable or terrifying, but he seems to have been a better than average soldier, and was twice promoted, first to corporal and then to sergeant.

In February 1917 he was watching the demonstration of a new **mortar** when it blew up. Five men were killed, and Mussolini himself was lucky to survive. He was thrown to the ground with over 40 pieces of metal in his body and spent many weeks in hospital. Afterwards he was fond of telling everyone how terribly he had suffered for his country, and when he went back to his newspaper job he carried on using his crutches for longer than he really needed to.

▲ Mussolini as a soldier in the trenches on the Italian–Austrian front.

The wounded hero

'He was so exhausted he could scarcely speak. He smiled out at us from his pale face, his eyes sunken in great hollows. His lips scarcely moved; one could see how horribly he had suffered.'

(Mussolini's girlfriend Margherita Sarfatti, after visiting him in hospital in 1917)

The soldiers' friend

The Italian war-effort had been badly managed, and Mussolini was quick to blame his traditional enemies – government and big business – for the failures. His newspaper supported the returning soldiers, who he thought deserved a better deal. Italy needed a **dictator**, he said in February 1918, 'a man who is ruthless and energetic enough to make a clean sweep'. He was, of course, talking about himself.

When the war ended in November the government behaved much as Mussolini had said it would. The soldiers were not given the jobs or the land they had been promised. There was not enough medical treatment for the injured, not enough **war pensions** for the families of the dead. And to make matters even worse, it began to seem as if the soldiers had fought and died for nothing. The British and the French broke their secret promises to Italy – they did not hand over any German **colonies** – and the country's territorial gains were much less than expected. Mussolini was quick to jump on the bandwagon. Italy had been cheated of her 'booty', he said.

5 The rise of Fascism

After the war many ex-soldiers had formed themselves into organized groups, and Mussolini became a leading member of one group in Milan. In March 1919 he went a step further, forming what he called a *Fasci di Combattimento* (a fighting group) of around 200 men. The word *fasci*, from which **Fascism** would take its name, means 'a bundle', but in Italian history it refers to the bundle of sticks which officials of the Roman Empire carried to show that they stood for justice. Mussolini's group used the bundle of sticks as their logo. They also dressed in black shirts and adopted an outstretched arm as their salute. Their favourite weapons were the dagger and a long wooden club, a bit like a baseball bat, called a *manganello*. Mussolini became known as *il Duce*, the leader.

At the beginning it was easier to see what the Fascists were against than what they were for. Mussolini still hated the establishment – the upper classes, big business, the old politicians, the Church – but he now hated **Socialists** and foreigners as well. They had all failed Italy, he said, and his Fascists would fight them in every way they could.

Reign of terror

In 1920 *squadristi* or fighting squads sprang into existence, and big street fights between them and the Socialists happened almost daily in the towns and cities of Italy. Sometimes these battles were advertised in advance, and people warned to keep off the streets. But most of the time it was more like a campaign of terror. The Fascist groups would seize those whom they considered enemies and punish them by either beating them with their *manganellos* or forcing them to drink pints of **castor oil**. Men were chained naked to trees, women had their heads shaved. Many people were killed.

▲ *Mussolini with other Fascists in their black shirts in Rome. They waged a campaign of terror to gain power throughout Italy.*

In most cases the authorities turned a blind eye to this Fascist violence. Some were frightened and some were bribed, but most were simply told to do nothing by their superiors in government, who were more than happy to see the Socialists destroyed. Early in 1921 the Fascists formed themselves into an official party, and when elections were held in May of that year the government even suggested to Mussolini that their parties should join together to fight the election. More than 100 opponents of the Fascists were killed in the campaign, and Mussolini's party won 35 seats in the Italian parliament. He was now one of the most important men in the country.

He was not directly involved in the violence, but as leader of the Fascists he was the man most responsible for it. The worse things got, the better it was for him, because he could then say that Italy needed a strong man like himself to impose order. To make himself more acceptable to the majority of Italians, he began cleaning up his own image. He started shaving every day and dressing more conservatively, often wearing a suit and top hat. The last remnants of the Socialism which he had preached in his youth disappeared from his writings and speeches. He was careful not to offend big business or the king, and he even had a good word for the pope, who was a particularly influential figure in Catholic Italy.

His followers, meanwhile, continued to make trouble. In May 1922 an army of Fascists took over the town of Ferrara and then waged a reign of terror in the nearby countryside. The government did nothing, and when the Socialists called a **general strike** in protest, the Fascists played a big part in defeating it.

TO LOCATE FERRARA, SEE THE MAP OF ITALY ON PAGE 10.

The March on Rome

The Fascists were now the most powerful single group in the country and many of Mussolini's lieutenants thought that it was time to seize power. Mussolini himself was apparently unsure, but allowed himself to be convinced. 'Either the government is given to us or we shall seize it by marching on Rome,' he declared in early October 1922.

▶ *Mussolini (second from left) in Milan during the March on Rome, October 1922.*

▲ *Luigi Facta, Italian prime minister at the time the Fascists were waging their reign of terror.*

The march was organized, and four columns of Fascist *squadristi* were soon on their way to the Italian capital. Prime Minister Luigi Facta, who had finally realized that the Fascists posed a real threat to his government, wanted to use the regular army against them, but the king refused to let him. Mussolini, holed up in his Milan office with the police waiting outside, was afraid that he had gone too far, but he kept his nerve and refused to compromise. The gamble paid off. On 29 October 1922 the king invited him to become his new prime minister.

A surprise

'What a character!' (Rachele's response, on hearing that her husband had become prime minister)

6 Government

Once he had been appointed prime minister, Mussolini moved into a luxury hotel in Rome with his black-shirted bodyguards. Flushed with his success, he took great pleasure in talking to journalists. The secret of political success, he told one, was 'to keep your heart a desert,' because friendship might get in the way of the struggle for power. There was no right or wrong in politics, he said, only force. The journalist noticed that the only pictures in the room were of Mussolini himself.

He was not yet a **dictator**, however. There was still powerful opposition among the other political parties, and he cautiously included some of their members in his first government. Having done that, he then demanded that parliament give him complete control for a whole year. If they did not give it to him, he hinted, then the **Fascist** gangs would deal with them. Parliament agreed. Just in case they changed their minds Mussolini turned the *squadristi* into an official private army (the MVSN), and gave them orders to make life difficult for his opponents.

Popular measures

In the meantime, he set about making himself popular with the Italian people. He had something for everyone. There were shorter working hours for workers, reduced taxes for big business, and **compulsory** religious education (Catholicism) in schools. The country was more peaceful, now that the street battles between Fascists and **Socialists** had mostly ended. The economy was also doing better, though this was true throughout Europe and had little to do with Mussolini. In foreign affairs he had two successes. In 1923 an Italian was murdered on the Greek island of Corfu, and Mussolini forced Greece to pay compensation. Later that year he persuaded Yugoslavia to give up the disputed town of Fiume to Italy.

▲ *Mussolini attending an international conference in Lausanne during his first month as prime minister, November 1922.*

After several terrible years it seemed that the outlook for Italy was improving, and many Italians gave their new leader most of the credit for the change. But Mussolini was taking no chances. The Grand Council of Fascism, which he set up as a sort of **think-tank**, proposed that in the next election the most successful party should only need 25 per cent of the vote to be given 66 per cent of the seats in parliament.

This new rule was accepted by the members of parliament, mostly because armed Fascists were watching to see how each of them voted.

The Fascists were now almost certain to win a big majority in the 1924 election, and their widespread use of violence and cheating during the campaign was probably unnecessary. The official result gave them 65 per cent of the vote, and Mussolini claimed a great victory.

He must have felt more secure knowing that both parliament and his party were now behind him, but he did not allow himself to relax or to become part of the old establishment, which he had always hated. During this period he worked hard at his office, worked hard at keeping himself fit, worked hard at chasing women. He remained unconventional, forgetting to shave for important occasions, wearing unfashionable clothes. His wife Rachele and the children did not join him in Rome for several years, but even when they did he carried on much as before. She said she didn't mind, that men were like that.

The murder of Matteotti

A few weeks after the 1924 election, the Socialist member of parliament Giacomo Matteotti made an angry speech in parliament accusing Mussolini of fixing the vote. A week later Matteotti mysteriously disappeared, and three months after that his body was found in a wood some way from the city.

There was no actual evidence connecting Mussolini to the murder, but few people in Italy had any doubt that he had given the order. His popularity dipped dramatically, and for several months it seemed possible that he would have to resign. 'My position is impossible,' he himself said. 'No one can remain in power with a corpse under his feet.'

Mussolini was shocked out of his dithering by a visit from other Fascist leaders, who told him that he must either take a real grip on the country or they would find someone else who would. On 3 January 1925 he made a speech to parliament in which he vowed to clean up both his own party and the country as a whole. He would become a dictator, he said, in order to give Italy the 'peace and quiet, work and calm' it needed. He would give it these things 'with love if possible and with force if necessary'.

Building a dictatorship

Over the next two years he made good this boast. In 1925 he ended freedom of the press, replaced the last few elected local government officials with Fascists, and reduced the powers of the king to interfere in politics. In 1926 he banned all political parties but his own and abolished the **trade unions**. In 1927 he set up a political police force (the OVRA) to make sure that there was no effective **underground opposition**.

By the end of the 1920s the only other man in Italy with any real power was the pope, and Mussolini reached a deal with him, the Lateran Treaty, in 1929. The Catholic Church received financial compensation for the land it had lost 60 years earlier during the **unification** of the country, and Catholicism was officially recognized as the **state religion**. In return Mussolini was given the pope's blessing. Catholics could now worship both men with an easy conscience, and Mussolini's popularity soared.

He had now bought off, decisively weakened or killed every possible opponent of his rule in Italy. And his changes to the laws meant that he could no longer be removed by legal means, only by force.

▲ *Mussolini and Pope Pius XI sign the Lateran Treaty between the Italian state and the Vatican, February 1929.*

Key dates: Mussolini's rise to power

1922	• October	The March on Rome
1924	• June	The murder of Matteotti
1925	• January	Mussolini's famous speech promising Italy 'peace and quiet'
	• June	The ending of freedom of the press
1926	• October	The banning of other political parties

7 Fascism for everyone

By 1926–27 the streets of Italy were full of portraits of Mussolini and slogans proclaiming, 'Mussolini is always right'. He encouraged this hero worship and spent many hours checking that his public image was the one he wanted. He praised himself in the articles he wrote for newspapers and made sure that he always looked strong and commanding in the photographs that were released to the media. The newspapers often mentioned how hard he worked, and the light was left on in his office to make people think he was still there. School textbooks were rewritten to make him appear almost super-human. 'The eyes of the *Duce* are on every one of you,' one textbook said.

But what was he actually doing for the Italian people? How was he dealing with the economy? Mussolini's approach to Italy's economic problems was to deal with them one by one in dramatic campaigns or 'battles'. He refused to look at the whole picture, and as a result his apparent successes were often really failures.

Mussolini's 'battles'

The 'Battle for Wheat' was a good example. Mussolini was determined to raise Italian wheat production, and so reduce Italy's need to buy foreign wheat. He succeeded in doing this, but Italian wheat was more expensive to grow than foreign wheat was to buy, so the country actually lost out as a result.

Other 'battles' were just as unsuccessful. The 'Battle over the Southern Problem' was meant to reduce poverty in the south of the country. It began with the building of a new model village in Sicily called Mussolinia, but was soon forgotten.

The 'Battle for Births' was supposed to increase Italy's population, and provide Mussolini with more men for his army. Single men had to pay higher taxes, while families with six or more children received tax relief. Mothers of seven children were given medals. But despite all these efforts the birth rate continued to fall throughout Mussolini's years in power.

The 'Battle for Land' was intended to create more farmland by draining marshes and clearing woodlands. The draining of the Pontine Marshes near Rome was a well-publicized success, but there were few others. In many ways these 'battles' were more like publicity stunts than real efforts to change things. Mussolini was always being photographed and filmed helping with the harvest, cutting down trees, and presenting medals to the women who had the most children.

▲ *Mussolini inaugurates (opens) a new agricultural works near Aprilia in the Pontine Marshes.*

In one respect, though, Mussolini was quite successful. His government spent a lot of money on public projects like motorways and impressive new buildings, and this increased spending helped Italy to weather the **Great Depression** of the early 1930s better than many richer countries like Britain, France and Germany, where governments mistakenly cut back their public spending.

The corporations

Mussolini's one great economic idea was his creation of 22 'corporations'. These included everyone involved in a particular industry – workers, managers and owners. The workers were guaranteed certain things, like free Sundays (still far from universal in those days) and an annual paid holiday, and they were also supposed to help their employers in making important decisions about wages and prices. This sounded fair, but in fact the workers were represented by Fascist Party officials, and the employers, by paying large sums of money to the Fascists, were often allowed to do whatever they wanted. Like many of Mussolini's ideas, the corporations were something of a cheat. But they were definitely something new, and like the various 'battles' they gave the false impression that he was actually changing things.

Mussolini himself was not particularly interested in making Italians better off. That was the sort of ambition ordinary politicians had. He thought of himself as more special than that: a truly historic figure who would really change Italy and the world. And the first thing he had to change was the attitude of his fellow Italians. They had to become Fascists, every last one of them.

Turning Italians into Fascists

The children were the most important. They were the future
of Italy, and they had to be brought up as Fascists from an
early age. Young boys joined the 'Sons of the She Wolf' at the
age of around 6, and four years after that they joined the
Balilla, which was named after a small boy who threw a stone
at the Austrian occupiers of the north Italian port of Genoa in
1746. In these organizations they were taught discipline and
obedience and what it meant to be a Fascist. They wore black
shirts, and in the Balilla they were also given weapons training.
Girls had their own organizations, which hammered home the
message that a woman's place was in the home, preferably
with a lot of children.

▲ *A Balilla motorcycle corps.*

The Balilla creed

The young boys who joined the Balilla organization would have to recite the following statement of belief:

'I believe in Rome the Eternal, the mother of my country, and in Italy her eldest daughter, who was born in her virginal bosom by the grace of God; who suffered through the barbarian invasions, was crucified and buried; who descended to the grave and was raised from the dead in the 19th century; who ascended into Heaven in her glory in 1918 and 1922; who is seated on the right hand of her mother Rome; who for this reason shall come to judge the living and the dead. I believe in the genius of Mussolini, in our Holy Father Fascism, in the communion of its martyrs, in the conversion of Italians, and in the resurrection of the Empire.'

Adults were also subjected to continuous propaganda. There were slogans in the streets designed to encourage a war-like attitude – NOTHING HAS EVER BEEN WON IN HISTORY WITHOUT BLOODSHED! – and frequent parades and marches. With future wars in mind, adults were supposed to make sure they kept themselves fit, and even the older Fascist leaders were forced to set a good example by doing gymnastic exercises in public. Mussolini was frequently to be seen on newsreels playing tennis, riding horses or jogging to work with his fellow leaders.

The *Dopolavoro* (the National Institute for After-Work Hours) organized leisure activities. It controlled sports grounds, theatres, libraries, even brass bands, and made sure that everyone who used such facilities was doing so in a proper Fascist manner. In 1926 a Fascist **academy** was set up to make sure that foreign influences were removed from art, books and films. Nothing could be approved for sale or showing unless it was considered 100 per cent Italian.

Men and women

Mussolini had a very traditional view of women, and huge efforts were made to emphasize the different roles which males and females were supposed to play in Fascist Italy. 'War is to the male what

▲ Il Duce *on horseback.*

childbearing is to the female' was one of his favourite slogans, and both sexes were supposed to do their duty in this regard. The more children that were born, the more Fascist soldiers there would be. And just in case there should be any confusion between the sexes, mixed schools were abolished and women were banned from wearing trousers.

Mussolini certainly tried to change his fellow Italians, to make the men more like himself and the women more like his wife, who had little interest in the world beyond her home and family. For a time he was able to convince himself that he was succeeding – there was, after all, no one brave enough to tell him otherwise – but such an attempt was doomed to failure.

A foreign admirer

'If I were an Italian I would don the Fascist Black Shirt.'
(Future British prime minister Winston Churchill, speaking in 1927. At this point Churchill still considered Mussolini a hero in the struggle against Communism.)

Il Duce – the Leader

After ten years in power Mussolini remained a popular leader. The Italian people were not, of course, being told the whole truth about how their country was doing, but there was a general feeling that things were getting better. Italy was taken more seriously abroad, and at home there was less trouble on the streets and in the factories. It seemed to many people that the benefits of having a strong leader more than made up for the loss of a few freedoms.

Mussolini encouraged such feelings in his many personal appearances. This was the leader that most Italians knew – the man helping with the harvest, the figure on the balcony with the grand gestures. He was a wonderful public speaker. His voice was powerful and attractive, and he did not talk down to his audience. He had the knack of making them feel that he and they were talking to each other.

The working day

Mussolini made many speeches from the balcony of the Palazzo Venezia in Rome, and it was in this building that he spent many of his working days. His office was in an enormous room called 'The Room of the Map of the World'.

◀ *Mussolini's palatial office in the Palazzo Venezia.*

Mussolini's desk was 4 metres long, and visitors had lots of time to appreciate how impressive it was as they took the long walk from one end of the room to the other.

His days usually began with physical exercises. After breakfast he went in to the office, where he spent the morning reading newspapers and government reports. In the afternoon he gave interviews to a wide variety of visitors – industrialists and musicians, sportsmen and foreign politicians. In the evening he usually went back to his Rome apartment. He liked at least nine hours' sleep each night and rarely stayed up late.

TO LOCATE THE PLACES MENTIONED, SEE THE MAP OF ITALY ON PAGE 10.

Family life

Mussolini's wife, Rachele, and the children did not move to Rome until he had been prime minister for five years – before that he had visited them in Milan three or four times a year. When they did move, it was mostly because he wanted to hold up his family as an example to the country.

▲ *The Mussolini family; from left to right: Rachele, Anna Maria, Romano, Benito, Edda, Bruno and Vittorio.*

Mussolini's children

Edda, b.1910

Vittorio, b.1916

Bruno, b.1918

Romano, b.1927

Anna Maria, b.1929

Rachele later claimed that he had been a good husband and father, but she probably did not expect very much. They may have liked and even respected each other, but he behaved more like a single man than a husband. It was said that he loved playing games with his five children; however, in later life one of his sons claimed that he had hardly ever seen his father when he was growing up. Mussolini certainly spent more time with his girlfriends, some of whom, like Margherita Sarfatti and Clara Pettaci, stayed with him for many years. The only man he was close to was his brother Arnaldo, who was now the editor of *Il Popolo d'Italia*.

Contempt

'To govern [Italians] you need only two things: policemen, and bands playing in the streets.'

(Mussolini to a friend, date unknown)

Mussolini and people

At heart, Mussolini really did not like people very much. He thought everyone was just out for themselves, and that those who claimed differently were either fooling themselves or trying to fool others. He thought religion was a sham, and when he was a young man he called priests 'black germs'. Although he later thought it wise to strike a deal with the pope – a wise move in a very Catholic country – he never really wavered from these views.

But he was superstitious. He thought it was dangerous to let the rays of the moon shine on his face when he was sleeping, and the drawers of his desk were full of good luck charms that admirers had given him, which he was afraid to throw away. He liked to try and make sense of his dreams, and was fond of reading other people's fortunes with a pack of cards.

Mussolini's low opinion of humanity was not immediately obvious, and most people who met him during his first ten years in power found him to be a charming and fascinating man. He was clever, he had a good memory, and he had a wide range of interests. He loved outdoor pursuits like riding, sailing, flying and playing tennis, but he also thought of himself as an intellectual, reading and writing a great deal.

▶ *Mussolini with his violin at one of his villas, around 1925.*

He played the violin quite well and he enjoyed listening to opera, classical symphonies and marches. He liked both serious literature and cheap fiction, and once said how upset he was that **Fascism** had failed to produce a single great poet. The visual arts, on the other hand, mostly left him cold. He called the famous tapestries of the Vatican Museum 'just bits of material' and said that he never visited an art gallery unless he had to. He preferred watching Laurel and Hardy comedies in his private cinema.

Mussolini had never been very interested in money, even in the early days when he had very little. His family lived simply, his children went to state schools, and he rarely gave his girlfriends presents. In the 1920s he often wore the same suit for weeks on end, and for many years he refused to take his prime minister's salary, saying that he already earned enough from his writings to satisfy his limited needs. On the other hand, when he wanted something special – like the private cinema or a brand new sports car – he could just order one for himself. He had his own plane, a yacht, and a private zoo in the grounds of one of his several villas. Cats were his favourite animals, and at one time he kept a mountain lion in his room on a leash.

Il Duce up close

'Short in stature, but with an air of great authority, his massive head conveyed an impression of great strength of character. He handled people like a man accustomed to having his orders obeyed, but displayed immense charm... . Mussolini was calm, dignified, and appeared the complete master of whatever subject was being discussed.'

(German vice-chancellor Franz von Papen, after meeting Mussolini in 1933)

Health and isolation

Mussolini was always keen to portray himself as a man of action, but for most of his adult life he was in bad health. His digestion had given him trouble since his time in Switzerland and as he grew older he was often in great pain from stomach ulcers. He gave up both alcohol and tobacco in the early 1920s and for long periods he was restricted to a liquid diet of milk and fruit juices. The Italian people were not told about any of this, or about the glasses he now needed to wear. Newspapers were forbidden from mentioning his age.

It seems possible that this continual ill health affected his mind, making him care even less about his fellow human beings. The death of his brother Arnaldo in 1932, the only other man whom he really seemed to care about, may have had the same effect. But the most important reason for his lack of caring was his own success. He was now so far above the ordinary people that he had no real contact with anyone. Everyone told him what they thought he wanted to hear, so he grew increasingly out of touch with what was really going on. And the more out of touch he got, the more likely he was to make mistakes.

▶ *An issue of the magazine founded by Mussolini and edited by his brother Arnaldo. Arnaldo was one of the few people Mussolini was ever close to.*

Foreign adventures

Throughout the first thirteen years of his rule Mussolini pursued a cautious foreign policy. He believed that both Italy and Germany had been badly treated by the **Treaty of Versailles** peace-makers, but made no real effort to overturn the post-war arrangement. Rather, he carried on playing Italy's traditional role, balancing between Germany and the Western powers, Britain and France. If anything, he favoured the latter. He joined with them in opposing a German threat to Austria in 1934, and attended the anti-German conference at Stresa in April 1935.

A change of course

In the next few months everything changed. Throwing caution aside, Mussolini embarked on a series of overseas adventures

which would antagonize the Western powers and force him into a virtual alliance with Germany.

Why did he change his foreign policy so dramatically? For one thing, he probably hoped that adventures abroad would take his people's mind off their troubles at home. Despite his public spending policies, the economic depression of the early 1930s had taken a toll on Italy, and Mussolini's government, like most others around the world, had become increasingly unpopular as unemployment rose.

◀ *Il Duce assumes a characteristic pose as he speaks to soldiers departing for the 1935 attack on Abyssinia.*

There is little doubt that he also welcomed the opportunity to spread his military wings. After all, **Fascists** were fighters by definition. The 'prestige of nations' depended on 'their military glories and their armed power.' Mussolini was ambitious for both Italy and himself. He would turn the Mediterranean into an Italian sea, conquer other countries and lead a new Roman Empire.

Abyssinia (now Ethiopia) was the target he chose for his first conquest. It was the only independent state left in Africa, and it lay between Italy's two existing east African possessions. Its mountain areas were fertile enough to support many Italian **colonists**. There was even an element of revenge involved – in 1896 Italian troops had been humiliated by the Abyssinians at the Battle of Adowa. Such a war would be bound to rally the nation behind him.

Mussolini did not think he was taking a great risk. He was confident he could get away with attacking Abyssinia, just as the Japanese had got away with their invasion of Manchuria in 1931. Britain was the most likely source of opposition, and the Italian embassy in London assured Mussolini that the British would do nothing.

The Abyssinian war

On 2 October 1935 the Italian people listened to their leader's voice booming out of loudspeakers in hundreds of town and village squares, announcing the invasion. It was 'better to live for one day as a lion than a thousand years as a lamb,' he told the departing soldiers.

The war itself lasted only eight months, and would have been shorter if the Italian generals had not been so cautious. The Italians had planes, tanks and machine-guns; the Abyssinians, rifles, swords and spears. Mussolini's oldest son Vittorio, who took part in the campaign as a pilot, wrote that 'it was magnificent sport … exceptionally good fun'. Not surprisingly the Abyssinians thought differently, particularly when they became the first non-European nation to have poison gas used against them.

The Abyssinian emperor appealed to the League of Nations to stop Italy. A few **economic sanctions** were introduced, but there was no attempt to include any, such as an **oil embargo**, which might really hurt the Italian war effort. The only effect of sanctions in Italy was to make the Western powers unpopular. They already had their empires, many Italians thought – why could they not let Italy have one too?

Victory made Mussolini more popular than ever among his own people. When the **Spanish Civil War** began a few months later he had no doubts about sending his troops off on a second adventure. There were some good reasons for helping Franco and his Fascist regime. Italy might be granted naval bases in return, and the mere existence of a third Fascist state in Europe could only benefit Mussolini and Italy. But his main reason for intervention was probably more basic. Having tasted one foreign success, he was simply hungry for more.

The invisible enemy

'Some were blinded. When others saw the burns spread upon their arms and legs and felt the increasing pain, whose source and end they could not understand, and for whose cure they had no medicine, Imru's men broke and fled.'

(An eyewitness to the December 1935 battle of Adi Quala, in which poison gas was used by the Italians)

▲ *Abyssinian troops, whose rifles were no match for the planes, tanks and machine guns used by Mussolini's Italian troops during the 1935 invasion.*

Relations with Hitler and Germany

Italy's relations with Germany before 1935 were not very good. When Hitler and the **Nazis** came to power in 1933, Mussolini was more worried about their attitudes to Austria than pleased by the fact of another Fascist triumph. His first impressions of Hitler were far from favourable. 'I don't like the look of him,' was his comment when they finally met in 1934. Later in the same visit he remarked to his aides that Hitler was 'a silly little clown' and 'quite mad'. The Nazis were not true Fascists, he thought. On the contrary, they had 'ruined our idea'.

The fall-out from the Abyssinian conquest may not have changed the way Mussolini felt about Hitler and the Germans, but it certainly altered his political calculations. The British and

FOR DETAILS ON KEY PEOPLE OF MUSSOLINI'S TIME, SEE PAGES 58–9.

▲ *Mussolini and Adolf Hitler reviewing German troops during the Italian leader's visit to Germany, September 1937.*

French had been against him, the Germans sympathetic. In Spain his troops and airmen were fighting alongside the Germans in support of Franco's Fascists.

Circumstances seemed to be forcing the two nations together, and in late 1936 Mussolini recognized this, declaring in a speech that a 'Rome–Berlin Axis' had been created, 'around which all European states that desire peace can revolve'. A month later Hitler told Mussolini's son-in-law and foreign minister, Count Ciano, that the *Duce* was 'the leading statesman in the world, to whom no other may remotely compare himself'.

Mussolini was flattered, as he was meant to be. In September of the following year he finally visited Germany, and was overwhelmed by the endless lines of steel-helmeted soldiers, the huge parades, the enormous factories, and the deafening crowds. Near the end of his tour he addressed a crowd of almost a million people in Berlin, who stayed to listen and cheer despite a thunderstorm and the fact that few of them could hear what he was saying.

Mussolini was deeply impressed. The Germans had the organization and the fighting spirit that he had always admired, and during this trip he seems to have convinced himself that they were invincible. Italian interests, he decided, lay in a German alliance. 'When Fascism has a friend,' he told the Berlin crowd, 'it will march with that friend to the last.'

Key dates: Mussolini abroad

1935	• April	Stresa Conference
	• October	Italy invades Abyssinia
1936	• May	Capture of the Abyssinian capital, Addis Ababa
	• July	Italian intervention in the Spanish Civil War begins
	• September	Mussolini announces a 'Rome–Berlin Axis'
1937	• September	Mussolini's first visit to Germany

Mussolini returned from his visit to Germany determined to make his own country more like Hitler's. He decided that the Italian army would adopt the German army's 'goose step' march and, much more seriously, he introduced anti-Jewish laws like those that already existed in Germany. Jews were forbidden to marry non-Jews, and they were not allowed to be teachers, bankers, journalists or lawyers.

Losing popularity at home

Most Italians disliked these new measures. They thought the goose step was ridiculous, and the anti-Jewish laws both ludicrous and cruel. Mussolini himself had no real desire to persecute the Jews but he was determined to demonstrate his support for Germany. When Hitler took over Austria in March 1938 Mussolini said and did nothing, even though he had once promised that he would never allow such a thing to happen. Now he denied ever saying this, which the Italian people knew was a lie. His constant talk of war also made them nervous. In a few short months his popularity fell sharply.

Mussolini knew that Italians did not like his friendship with the Germans but he did not care. He was bored with his own country, which he felt he had already conquered. Now he was interested in new conquests, in the world outside Italy. He also realized that his and Hitler's greed would probably lead to a major war, and most of the time he welcomed the fact. For one thing, Italians would have the chance to prove that they were true **Fascists**. For another, he was sure that Italy would make **territorial gains**. However, he also knew that Italy would not be ready to fight a war for several years. So he had to be cautious, to make sure he picked the right time.

Trying to keep up with Hitler

The problem was, the Germans were in such a hurry, and he did not want to be left behind. When Hitler threatened Czechoslovakia in September 1938 a conference was called at Munich, and Mussolini had little trouble persuading the British and French to let Hitler have his way without war. He received a hero's welcome when he returned to Italy. He liked being popular again, but he hated the reason for it. He was furious when the crowd shouted out that he was an 'angel of peace'. The character of the Italian people, he said angrily, must be 'moulded by fighting'.

Mussolini spent most of the following winter worrying about what he should do when the inevitable war came. Basically, he wanted to share in any German successes without taking any risks. When Hitler took over the rest of Czechoslovakia early in 1939, Mussolini responded by taking over Albania. There was no risk in this, because Albania had been a virtual Italian **colony** for several years.

In May 1939 German promises of support for eventual Italian conquests of Yugoslavia and Greece persuaded Mussolini to sign the Pact of Steel, which committed Germany and Italy to support each other in attacks on other states. But only days later Mussolini made sure to tell the Germans that Italy could not consider a war for at least four years.

◄ Mussolini, Hitler, the French leader Edouard Daladier and British Prime Minister Neville Chamberlain at the Munich Conference, 1938.

▲ *Mussolini with his sons Bruno and Vittorio on the eve of World War II.*

On the sidelines

The Germans had no intention of waiting that long, and in August 1939 they attacked Poland. England and France declared war on Germany, but Mussolini did not bring Italy in on Germany's side. He wanted to, he told Hitler, but he could only do so if the Germans sent him 17,000 train-loads of supplies. This, he knew very well, was quite impossible.

He dithered throughout the first nine months of the war, but when, in May 1940, the German army swept through Belgium, Holland and France, he realized that it was now or never. If he stayed out any longer the Germans would get all the booty, and Italy would be left with nothing.

He just could not resist the temptation. When Pietro Badoglio, Chief Marshal of the army told him that there were not enough shirts for his troops, let alone weapons, he replied that all he needed was 'a few thousand dead', so that he could 'sit at the peace table with the victor' and claim his share of the spoils.

On 10 June 1940 Mussolini declared war on France and Britain. It was the biggest mistake of his life.

The fatal thrust

'On this tenth day of June, the hand that held the dagger has stuck it in the back of its neighbour.'

(US President Roosevelt, speaking of Italy's declaration of war on France)

FOR DETAILS ON KEY PEOPLE OF MUSSOLINI'S TIME, SEE PAGES 58–9.

◀ *King Victor Emmanuel III and Mussolini during military manoeuvres in the Abruzzi mountains, 1938.*

Commander-in-chief

Mussolini took Italy into World War II without consulting either his close advisers or the Grand **Fascist** Council. There was no chance for anyone to point out all the reasons why this was such a terrible decision.

Unwilling and unready

The Italian people did not want to go to war, and particularly not on the side of the Germans. Even if they had been enthusiastic, the country's armed forces were completely unready. Mussolini had talked about the coming war for years, but had done hardly anything to prepare for it. He claimed that Italy now grew enough wheat to feed its people, but forgot that the farmers still had to buy their fertilizer from abroad. He said that Italy was producing enough steel to make weapons, but forgot that the steelworks relied on imported coal to make the steel. There were not enough uniforms for the soldiers, and the weaponry was often outdated. There were hardly any tanks.

Mussolini refused to discuss his military plans with either the Germans or his own commanders. They assumed that his main aim would be to drive the British out of the Mediterranean, and that the first step would be to capture the island fortress of Malta, but there were no plans to mount these or any other attacks. Instead of acting, Mussolini behaved like a child in a sweet shop who couldn't decide which sweets he wanted. Should he attack Egypt? Or Yugoslavia? Or somewhere else? Or perhaps several places at once? There was no military calculation in all this. He was simply wondering which new conquests would impress the world most.

▲ *Mussolini reviews his Eighth Army in December 1940.*

Disasters everywhere

In the end Mussolini ordered two major attacks, one into
Egypt from the Italian **colony** of Libya, the other into Greece
from Albania. Both were disasters. The attack into Egypt was
beaten back by a much smaller British force, and thousands of
Italians were taken prisoner. The attack on Greece, which
began in late autumn, was bungled just as badly. There were no
suitable ports in Albania for landing the Italian troops and
there were no good maps. The reluctant Italian troops, who
had only been issued with light uniforms and cardboard shoes,
soon found themselves fighting a losing battle against the
determined Greeks in snow-covered mountains.

Cold treatment

*'This snow and cold are very good. In this way our good-for-
nothing Italians, this mediocre race, will be improved. One of
the principle reasons I wanted the Apennines to be reforested
was because it would make Italy colder and snowier.'*

(Mussolini, December 1939)

The invasion of Greece

'Hitler always presents me with a fait accompli *[something already done]. This time I am going to pay him back in his own coin. He will find out from the papers that I have occupied Greece.'*

(Mussolini, October 1940)

Hitler, who had warned Mussolini against attacking Greece, was furious, and with good reason. He had to postpone his invasion of Russia by several crucial weeks in order to come to the Italians' aid.

In early 1941 the Italian navy suffered a terrible defeat off the Greek coast near Cape Matapan, and Abyssinia was conquered by British troops from East Africa. Almost all of the local troops serving with the Italian army in Abyssinia chose to **desert** rather than fight, which showed how unpopular Italian rule was.

Mussolini's first year as a war leader had been a complete failure, and in both Greece and North Africa he had only been saved from defeat by German help. Mussolini, who had been the first Fascist head of state, and who until recently had still seen himself as at least Hitler's equal, was now clearly a very junior partner in the alliance. It was humiliating.

In private he grew more and more critical of Hitler and the Germans. When they attacked Russia in June 1941 he was appalled. 'This means the war is lost,' he confided to his wife, but in public he remained the ever-faithful ally, and even insisted on sending Italian divisions to fight on the Russian front. Very few men returned.

▲ *Italian troops on duty at an anti-aircraft post on the Russian front. They were unused to the cold climate, and many suffered from frostbite.*

At home in Italy his remaining popularity was fast disappearing. Soldiers home on leave spread the news of how badly everything was organized at the front. In the shops there were increasing shortages of many things, including food. More and more Italian men were being forced to take jobs in Germany's war industries, and the poor treatment they received there was greatly resented. British and American bombing of Italian cities increased the misery.

Things improved slightly at the end of 1941. Italian midget submarines launched a dramatic attack on British ships in Alexandria harbour, and for a while it seemed as if the British might be beaten in North Africa by the Italians and their German allies. In the summer of 1942 Mussolini travelled across the Mediterranean, hoping that he could make a triumphal entry into Cairo, but his army's advance was halted and he had to return home disappointed.

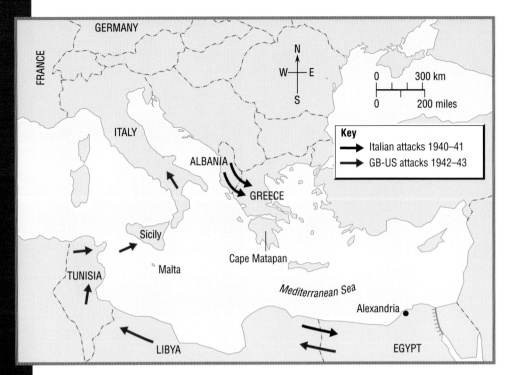

▲ *Italy at war, 1940–43.*

Refusing the blame

During the war Mussolini's health again grew worse. The death of his son Bruno in a flying accident in 1941 and the frequent setbacks on the military front brought back the terrible stomach pains of earlier years and he was often in great pain. During January 1943, when the last important battles were being fought in North Africa, he rarely got out of bed. Even on better days he had violent mood swings and often seemed incapable of making up his mind.

As defeat followed defeat Mussolini blamed everyone but himself. He called his commanders incompetent and conveniently forgot that he had appointed them. He blamed the Italian people, who were 'a race of sheep', 'soft and unworthy', a people 'made flabby by art'. It never seems to have occurred to him that they fought badly because they did not believe in what they were fighting for.

12 Defeat

In July 1943 British and American armies landed in Sicily, and it was clear that an Italian defeat was now just a matter of time. When Mussolini's worried subordinates called a meeting of the **Fascist** Grand Council later that month they were shocked to see how ill he looked, and appalled by his complete lack of ideas for dealing with the crisis. A vote was passed sacking him as prime minister and commander-in-chief. Mussolini expected the king to overturn this decision, but to his great surprise the king arrested him instead.

After brief spells of imprisonment on two Mediterranean islands he was taken to an empty ski resort hotel in the Apennines, high on the Gran Sasso plateau. There he played cards and gossiped with his guards for several weeks, until German paratroopers led by Otto Skorzeny (see page 59) suddenly dropped out of the sky to rescue him.

TO LOCATE THE PLACES MENTIONED, SEE THE MAP OF ITALY ON PAGE 10.

During Mussolini's weeks of imprisonment the king and his new government had made a deal with the British and Americans to drop out of the war. The Germans had retaliated by occupying north and central Italy, and they now wanted Mussolini to rule these areas for them. He soon found out that he would be just a puppet ruler – one without any real power. He was only allowed to live in the northern town of Gargagno, close to the German border, not in Rome.

▶ *Mussolini set free by German paratroopers.*

Mussolini may have wondered whether it was worth it, but he really had no other choices.

At least his health improved. His new German doctor realized that the huge quantities of milk that Mussolini had always drunk to help his stomach had actually made things worse. He was put on a new diet, and for the first time in many years he was mostly free of pain.

A German puppet

The Germans allowed Mussolini to have his revenge on those who had voted against him in July. Several were shot, including his own son-in-law, Count Galeazzo Ciano (see page 58). Mussolini's daughter Edda, who had once been his favourite, never forgave him for killing her husband.

His wife, Rachele, was also angry with him. She had just learned about his ten-year affair with Clara Petacci, whom the Germans had thoughtfully brought to live nearby. Mussolini failed to keep his promise to break off relations with Clara, despite Rachele's angry pleas.

In some ways he now seemed a rather pathetic figure. He still blamed everyone else for his problems and he was as ready as ever to ignore the rights of other human beings.

◀ *Clara Petacci in 1942. Her affair with Mussolini had begun in 1936.*

Many Italians had taken up arms against the German occupation, and he gave orders that ten of these **partisans** should be shot for each Fascist killed. He also made no attempt to stop the German deportation of Italy's Jews, even though he now knew that millions were being killed in German concentration camps.

Death

After landing in Sicily, the British and Americans had slowly pushed the Germans back up the Italian peninsula. By early 1945 most of the country was liberated, and in April Mussolini joined a retreating German convoy heading north across the Alps. It was stopped by partisans, who found him hiding in one of the lorries, wearing a German uniform. The next day he was shot, along with Clara, who had refused to leave his side. His last words were: 'Shoot me in the chest.' Their bodies were taken to Milan and hung up by the heels in a town square, the Piazzale Loreto.

▲ The bodies of Mussolini, Clara Petacci and other captured Fascists hang in the Piazzale Loreto in Milan.

Impact and legacy

Few men had more chance to influence the course of events during their lifetime than Benito Mussolini, and few did less to further the cause of human happiness. In Italy his word was law for more than twenty years, but in the aftermath of his fall it was hard to find a single one of his countrymen who had a good thing to say about him.

▲ *A typical image of* il Duce *in his prime.*

During his lifetime

In the early days Mussolini did have a number of achievements to his name. He restored the domestic peace that his own party had helped to destroy; he made Italians feel better about their country; he healed the long rift between the Italian state and the pope. But in the process he replaced a far from perfect democracy with an often brutal **dictatorship**, and eventually led Italy into a war which left the country in ruins, millions dead or bereaved, and its Jewish population decimated.

His influence outside Italy was completely negative. In its early years his government gave **Fascism** an air of respectability, and so encouraged the rise of the more dangerous **Nazis** in Germany. His invasion of Abyssinia brought war and mass murder to Africa and fatally weakened the **League of Nations**. His intervention in the **Spanish Civil War** helped condemn Spain to 40 years of Fascism.

His most positive influential act was completely unintentional. His invasion of Greece was motivated by greed for glory and a childish desire not to be outshone by Hitler. It eventually caused a five-week delay in the German attack on Russia, and this delay may well have saved the Russians from defeat and the world from a Nazi victory.

After his death

Mussolini's influence since his death has been almost non-existent. Fascism, which he did more than anyone else to create, was completely discredited by its defeat in the war. There are politicians today who follow similar policies, but very few of them like to be called Fascists or associated with the names of Mussolini and his ally Hitler.

Wars are still being fought, but to glorify them — to believe, as Mussolini did, that they turn boys into men — now seems stupid and cruel. In much the same way, his attitudes to women seem old-fashioned and oppressive.

There is no doubt that Mussolini was an extraordinary man, but he was not a good one. His one great achievement was to win power and hold on to it, but the only one to really gain from that power was himself.

Timeline

1883	Benito Mussolini is born.
1892	Is sent away to school.
1901	Finishes school.
1902	Has his first teaching job. Travels to Switzerland.
1904	Returns to Italy to do military service.
1905	His mother dies.
1906	Is released from the army, and goes north to take another teaching job.
1907	Returns to the Romagna region.
1908	Gets involved in farming disputes, goes to prison for a short time, and gets engaged to Rachele. Teaches in the Trentino region of Austria.
1909	Expelled from Austria.
1910	First child (Edda) is born.
1912	Mussolini leads the protest against the Libyan War in Forli. Becomes editor of *Avanti!* in Milan.
1914	Outbreak of World War I. Mussolini leaves *Avanti!* and sets up *Il Popolo d'Italia*.
1915	Italy enters the war. Mussolini is called up. Marries Rachele.
1916	First son (Vittorio) is born.
1917	Mussolini is badly wounded in an explosion. Once recovered, returns to his newspaper in Milan.
1918	World War I ends. Second son (Bruno) is born.
1919	Mussolini forms the *Fasci di Combattimento*.
1920	The **squadristi** begin a two-year reign of terror.
1922	The March on Rome. Mussolini becomes prime minister.
1924	The **Fascists** win the election. The Socialist member of parliament Matteotti is murdered. 'Battle over the Southern Problem' begins.

1925	Mussolini ends freedom of the press.
	'Battle for Wheat' begins.
1926	All political parties exept the Fascist Party are banned.
1927	Mussolini sets up the OVRA political police.
	Third son (Romano) is born.
	Rachele and children join Mussolini in Rome.
1929	Mussolini agrees the Lateran Treaty with the pope.
	Second daughter (Anna Maria) is born.
1931	Mussolini's brother Arnaldo dies.
1934	First meeting with Hitler.
1935	The Stresa Conference. The invasion of Abyssinia.
1936	Victory in Abyssinia.
	The **Spanish Civil War** begins.
1937	Mussolini's first visit to Germany.
1938	Hitler takes over Austria.
	The Munich Conference.
1939	The Spanish Civil War ends.
	Italy invades Albania.
	Mussolini and Hitler sign the Pact of Steel.
	World War II breaks out when Hitler invades Poland.
1940	Italy joins the war against France and Britain, attacking both Greece and Egypt.
1941	Death of Mussolini's son Bruno.
1943	Italy is invaded by British and Americans after defeat in North Africa.
	Mussolini is forced from office, arrested, and then rescued by the Germans. He becomes head of a puppet government in North Italy.
1945	Mussolini is caught by Italian **partisans** and executed.

Key people of Mussolini's time

Badoglio, Pietro (1871–1956). Italian general (chief of staff, 1919–21, and from 1925) who played a significant role in the conquest of Abyssinia (1935–36). Badaglio was less than enthusiastic about Italy's participation in World War II, and was chosen to head the first non-**Fascist** government after Mussolini was overthrown in 1943.

Churchill, Sir Winston (1874–1965). Controversial British politician. During the 1930s Churchill spoke out against the timid policy of successive British governments. He became prime minister during the crucial early phase of World War II, and proved an inspirational figure in British defiance of Nazi Germany.

Ciano, Count Galeazzo (1903–44). Married Mussolini's daughter Edda in 1930 and thereafter enjoyed a meteoric rise. After a short spell as head of the government press office and service as a pilot in Abyssinia, Ciano was appointed foreign minister in 1936. Over the next few years he became one of Mussolini's closest confidants. His admiration for his father-in-law verged on hero-worship, but he neither liked nor trusted the Germans, and in the late 1930s argued in vain against a close alliance of the two countries. In 1944 he was executed for his involvement in Mussolini's overthrow.

Franco, Francisco (1892–1975). As an army general, Franco was one of the leaders of the revolt against the Spanish government that led to the **Spanish Civil War** (1936–39). In 1937 he became leader of the Falange (Fascist) Party. After winning the war he became **dictator** of Spain, and held that position until his death. In World War II he kept his country neutral, much to the indignation of fellow-Fascists Hitler and Mussolini.

Hitler, Adolf (1889–1945). Leader of the German National Socialist Party (1921–45) and Führer (dictator) of Germany from 1933 until he committed suicide in April 1945. Hitler restored the German economy and German pride through rearmament and an aggressive determination to retrieve territory lost in World War I. He was primarily responsible for the outbreak of World War II and the subsequent killing of six million Jews in German-occupied Europe.

Roosevelt, Franklin Delano (1882–1945). US president (1933–45), largely responsible for New Deal policies that helped to lift the US economy out of the **Great Depression**. In World War II, Roosevelt's willingness to supply Britain with economic and military assistance before the US was officially involved played an important role in the defeat of Nazi Germany.

Skorzeny, Otto (1908–75). German officer, famous for leading daring operations behind enemy lines during World War II. Skorzeny rescued Mussolini from captivity in 1943 and was also involved in the attempted capture of two other foreign leaders: he succeeded in kidnapping Hungary's Admiral Horthy but failed to capture the Yugoslav **partisan** leader Tito.

Victor Emmanuel III, King (1869–1947). Third king of Italy, who came to the throne when his father was assassinated in 1900. He chose to make Mussolini prime minister in 1922, and was happy to accept Fascism as long as it proved successful. He sacked Mussolini in 1943 when it became clear that Italy was defeated in World War II. He abdicated (resigned as king) in 1946, three weeks before Italians voted to abolish the monarchy.

Places to visit and further reading

Place to visit
Imperial War Museum, Lambeth Road, London SE1 6HZ

Websites
BBC history website:
www.bbc.co.uk/education/modern/fascism/fascihtm.htm
Detailed biographical article from the Grolier Online
Encyclopedia:
gi.grolier.com/wwii/wwii_mussolini.html
Educational website from the ThinkQuest Library of Entries:
library.thinkquest.org/17120/data/bio/mussolini
Educational website provided by the UK Public Records
Office:
learningcurve.pro.gov.uk/heroesvillains/mussolini
Heinemann Explore, an online resource for Key Stage 3
history:
www.heinemannexploresec.com
University of Wisconsin special collection on Italian Life Under
Fascism:
www.library.wisc.edu/libraries/dpf/Fascism

Further reading
Italy and Mussolini, Josh Brooman, Longman, 1985
Twentieth Century World (Living Through History series),
Nigel Kelly, Rosemary Rees and Jane Shuter, Heinemann
Library, 1998
Key Battles of World War II (20th Century Perspectives series),
Fiona Reynoldson, Heinemann Library, 2001

Sources
Benito Mussolini, Christopher Hibbert, Penguin, 1962
Italy Under Mussolini, Christopher Leeds, Wayland, 1972
Mussolini, Dennis Mack Smith, Weidenfeld and Nicholson, 1981
Mussolini and Fascist Italy, Marian Freeman, Bell & Hyman, 1984
The Brutal Friendship, F.W.D. Deakin, Penguin, 1966
The Rome–Berlin Axis, Elizabeth Wiskemann, Fontana, 1969

Glossary

abduction taking away by force

academy club of well-known scholars, artists and scientists

anti-clerical being opposed to religion and churches

anti-establishment being opposed to the people in power in a society, whether in government, business or culture

anti-militaristic being opposed both to war and to the powerful position of soldiers in peacetime

Austro-Hungarian Empire empire covering a large area in central and eastern Europe, which in 1914 included all or part of present-day Austria, Hungary, the Czech Republic, Slovakia, Poland, Romania, Bosnia, Croatia, Slovenia and Italy

authoritarian communist type of communist (someone who believes that all property should be owned by everyone) who believes that a dictatorship is necessary to enforce communist rules of ownership

blacksmith person who shapes iron by heating and hammering it, particularly into horseshoes

castor oil oil from the seeds of a tropical plant, used to treat constipation. In large amounts, it can make people vomit.

colony territory ruled by another, usually distant, country

compulsory when something has to be done, as ordered by government

desert abandon an army fighting unit

dictatorship government by an individual (dictator) or small group that does not allow the mass of the people any say

economic sanctions refusal to trade with another nation, either in one particular product or in all products

editor in newspaper and magazine publishing, person responsible for choosing which stories go into each edition and who writes them

Fascism dictatorial system of government originating in Italy, also used in Germany, known for its aggressive nationalism

general strike when workers in all industries refuse to work for a period of time

Great Depression period of great economic hardship that began around 1929 and lasted for most of the following decade. Most countries of the world were affected, but the seriousness of the Depression varied from country to country.

League of Nations international organization set up after the First World War to help settle disputes between nations

military service compulsory period of months or years spent in the armed forces, in either peace or war

mortar short, portable cannon for lobbing shells over short distances.

Nazis shortened term for members of the Nationalsozialistische Deutsche Arbeiterpartei (National Socialist German Workers' Party), led by Adolf Hitler, who ruled Germany from 1933 to 1945. Nazism was a type of Fascism notable for being both aggressively nationalistic and aggressively racist.

neutral supporting neither one side nor another in a dispute

oil embargo refusal by one nation to sell oil, or to allow oil to be sold, to another nation

partisans unofficial fighters, usually against occupying foreign troops

persecute make life very difficult for, cruelly ill-treat

poison gas disabling or lethal gas, manufactured for use in war

propaganda promotion of ideas, often involving a selective version of the truth

sabotage deliberate damage

socialist someone who believes in socialism. There are many types of socialism, but all of them stress the need for a political system that promotes equality between people and values the long-term needs of the community above the short-term needs of the individual.

Spanish Civil War war within Spain (1936–39) between republican government forces (mostly Socialists and Communists) and rebel Fascist forces. The German and Italian governments gave crucial military support to their victorious fellow Fascists.

squadristi Italian term for small, organized and unofficial groups of armed men

state religion official religion of a country

territorial gains land taken from one country by another

think-tank group of experts who discuss ideas and different ways to solve problems

trade union organized association of workers in a particular industry or profession, formed to protect its members' interests

Treaty of Versailles list of arrangements forced on the defeated Germany at the end of World War I

trenches long narrow ditches dug in the ground. In World War I thousands of miles of these were used to shelter soldiers from enemy fire and to attack from.

ulcer open sore on or in the body

underground opposition opponents of a government who try to keep their identity and whereabouts secret from that government

unification when several states join together to form a new, larger state. Italy became a single unified kingdom in 1861. Before that there were more than ten small states in the Italian peninsula.

war pension money paid to the dependants (wives, children) of those who have died in a war

Index

Titles in the *Leading Lives* series include:

Hardback   0 431 13851 6

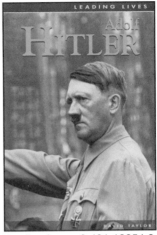

Hardback   0 431 13854 0

Hardback   0 431 13853 2

Hardback   0 431 13850 8

Hardback   0 431 13852 4

Hardback   0 431 13855 9

Find out about the other titles in this series on our website www.heinemann.co.uk/library